IN THE JUNGLE

STICKER ACTIVITY BOOK

Pull out the sticker sheets and keep
them by you as you complete each page.
There are also lots of extra stickers to
use in this book or anywhere you want!
Have fun!

NATIONAL GEOGRAPHIC
Washington, D.C.

Consultant: Richard Walker
Editorial, Design, and Production by
make believe ideas

Picture credits: All images Shutterstock unless noted as follows: **Gerry Ellis/NGS:** 1 br (chameleon), 6 bl,
38 m; ml, 39 tr, **Jak Wonderly/NGS:** 2 tl; bl, **Make Believe Ideas:** 3 br, 6 tr (red-eyed tree frog x2), 14 m,
19 tl; tr; m (bee x3), 26 br, 30 tm (tiger x5); bm, 37 l (tree), 40 br (macaw), **PhotoDisc/NGS:** 4 tm,
©Stephen Dalton/naturepl.com: 33 ml; mr.

Sticker pages: All images Shutterstock unless noted as follows: **Gerry Ellis/NGS:** 38, 39 white-handed gibbon,
Jak Wonderly/NGS: 12, 13 red-tailed boa, 40 blue-and-yellow macaw, **Make Believe Ideas:** 6, 7 red-eyed tree frog x3;
dinosaur; popsicle, 18, 19 bee x9, 30, 31 tiger x2; tiger cub, **Extra Stickers (Sheet 2)** tiger x2,
Extra Stickers (Sheet 3) red-eyed tree frog x6; baby tapir x2, **Matt Propert/NGS:** 14, 15 Malayan tapir,
©Stephen Dalton/naturepl.com: 32, 33 Wallace's flying frog (feet) x3.

Printed in China. 15/MBI/1

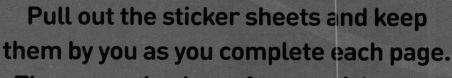

Birds fly through the jungle!

The map behind each page number tells you where the animals live. These animals live in Central and South America.

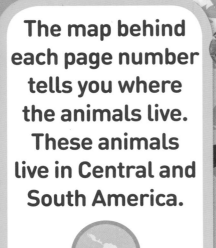

Jungles are tropical forests thick with plants and trees—and full of amazing animals!

Colorful birds, like macaws, live in the jungle.

Find the missing stickers. How many macaws can you count?

....

Help the hummingbirds
reach the flowers.

Start

Hummingbirds
drink nectar
from jungle
flowers.

red-and-green
macaw

Finish

Sticker more bugs!

3

Wild cats roam the rain forest.

The black spots covering a jaguar's fur are called rosettes.

Black jaguars have black spots, too!

Sticker a fierce face!

Help mommy jaguar find her cubs!

jaguar

4

Ocelots like to hide in trees!

Who is hiding?

(dot-to-dot puzzle, numbers 1–51)

Ocelots have both spots and stripes!

ocelot

Sticker and color the patterns, then create your own!

5

Frogs leap over leaves!

Find the missing stickers, then circle the one that doesn't belong in each group!

Bright red eyes help the red-eyed tree frog frighten attackers.

red-eyed tree frog

Leafcutter ants carry leaves many times their own weight!

Add stickers to see what the ants are carrying!

Some glass frogs have see-through bellies!

glass frogs

Draw what's inside the frog's belly!

Monkeys jump from tree to tree.

pygmy marmoset

Pygmy marmosets only weigh about as much as a stick of butter!

The noisy howler monkey uses its tail like an extra arm!

howler monkey

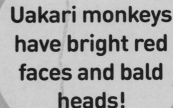

Uakari monkeys have bright red faces and bald heads!

Give the monkeys red faces!

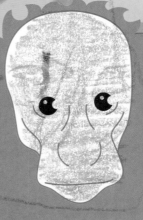

Find the missing stickers, then draw lines to match the monkey pairs.

uakari
monkey

Color the jungle plants.

pygmy
marmoset

howler
monkey

9

Sloths live upside down!

A sloth hangs upside down for most of its life. On the ground, it has to drag itself along with its claws!

Use the grid to draw the sloth!

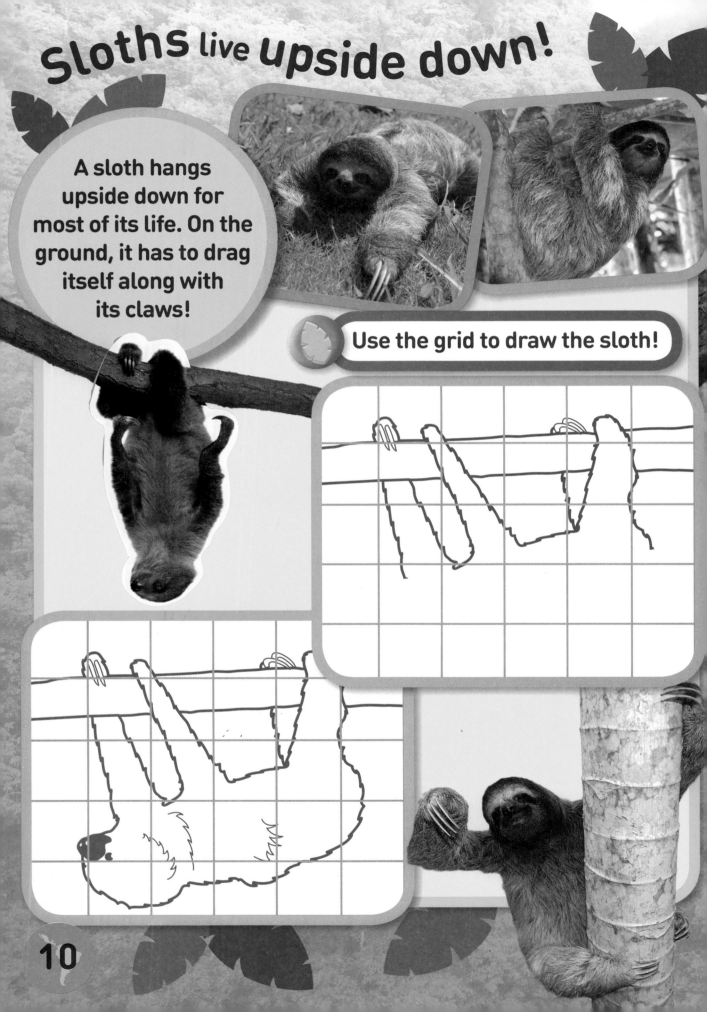

Sloths sleep more than 15 hours a day!

Find three differences between the pictures.

Use stickers to finish the sloth sums!

1 + 2 = 3

2 + 2 = 4

Bright boas slither and coil!

Adult emerald tree boas are green, but as babies, they are many colors!

Start

Finish

Help the snake get through the wiggly maze!

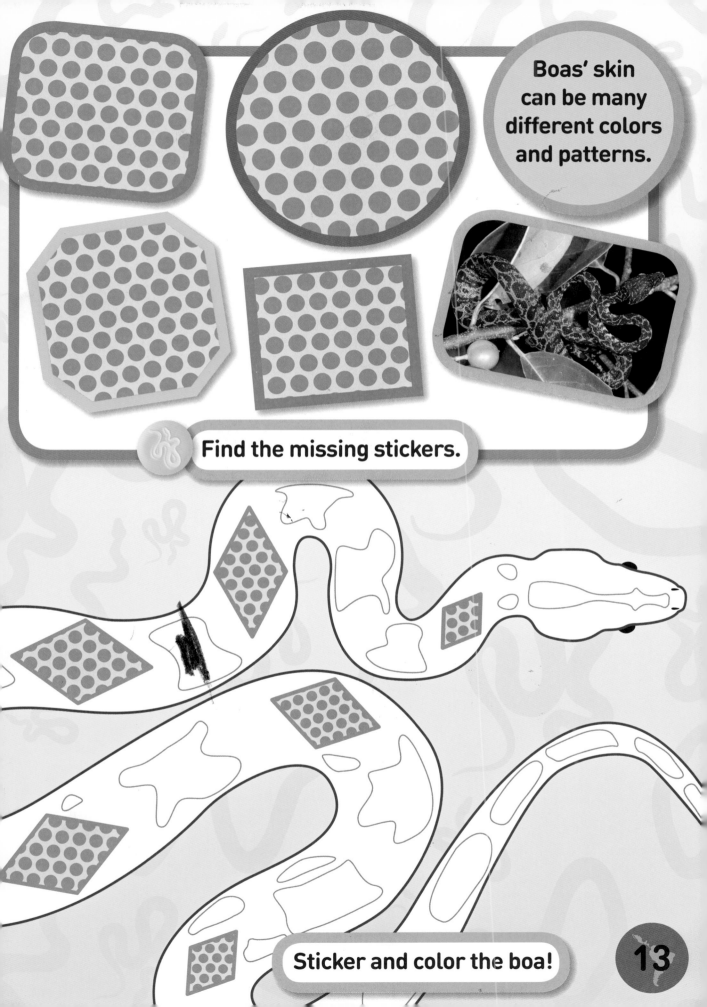

Boas' skin can be many different colors and patterns.

Find the missing stickers.

Sticker and color the boa!

13

Tapirs and Capybaras are cute!

All tapirs live in Central and South America, except the Malayan tapir, which lives in Asia.

Brazilian tapir

Malayan tapir

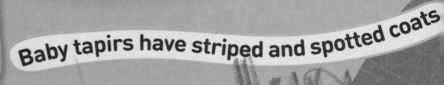

Baby tapirs have striped and spotted coats

Color the baby tapirs hiding in the jungle!

Capybaras live near the water in groups of up to 100!

Sticker the capybara family. How many can you count?

The capybaras are swimming. Sticker some fun swim gear!

Super snappers!

Caimans live in jungle swamps. The black caiman is the largest and the dwarf caiman is the smallest.

dwarf caiman

black caiman

Complete the caiman pictures!

Piranhas live in jungle rivers in groups of up to 100 fish!

A group of hungry piranhas could eat a cow!

Find the fish that's different!

Amazing African birds!

These animals live in Africa.

Turacos are poor fliers. Instead, they hop and run along the treetop branches.

Fischer's turaco

violet turaco

Sticker and color the jungle flowers!

18

Sticker more bee-eaters!

Bee-eaters fly through the jungle catching insects. They also like to sunbathe!

Follow the lines to see who finds a buzzing snack!

19

Mandrills find food on the jungle floor.

Start

Sticker a colorful snout!

Find your way through the termite maze!

Finish

20

Mandrills eat mostly plants and fruit, as well as bugs such as spiders and termites.

Stickers for pages 10 and 11

Stickers for pages 12 and 13

Extra stickers

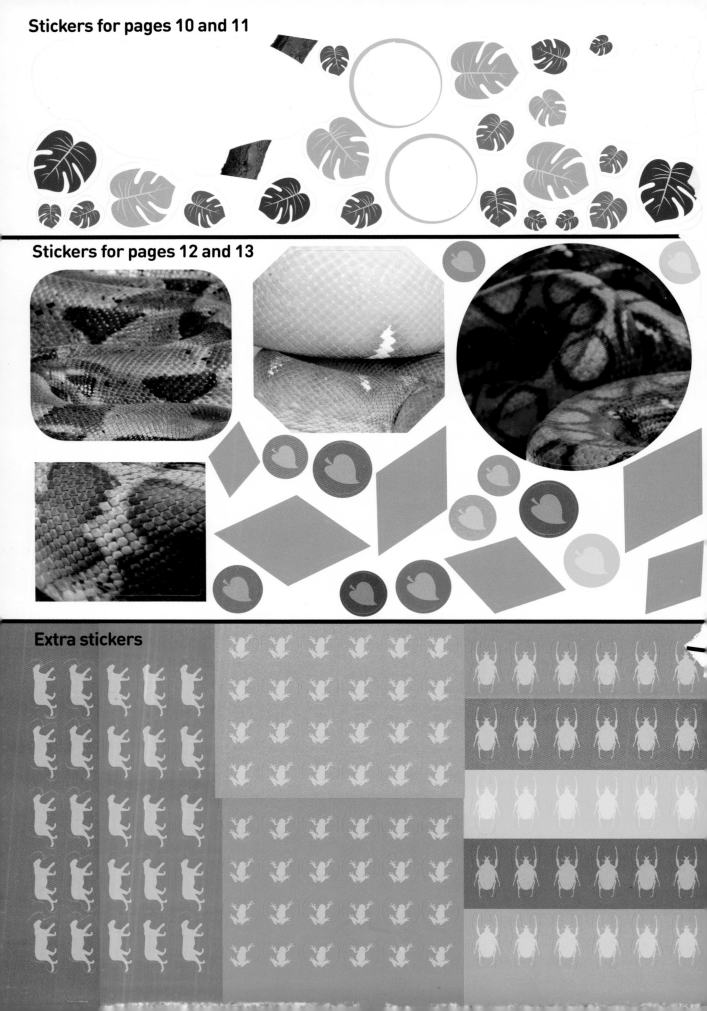

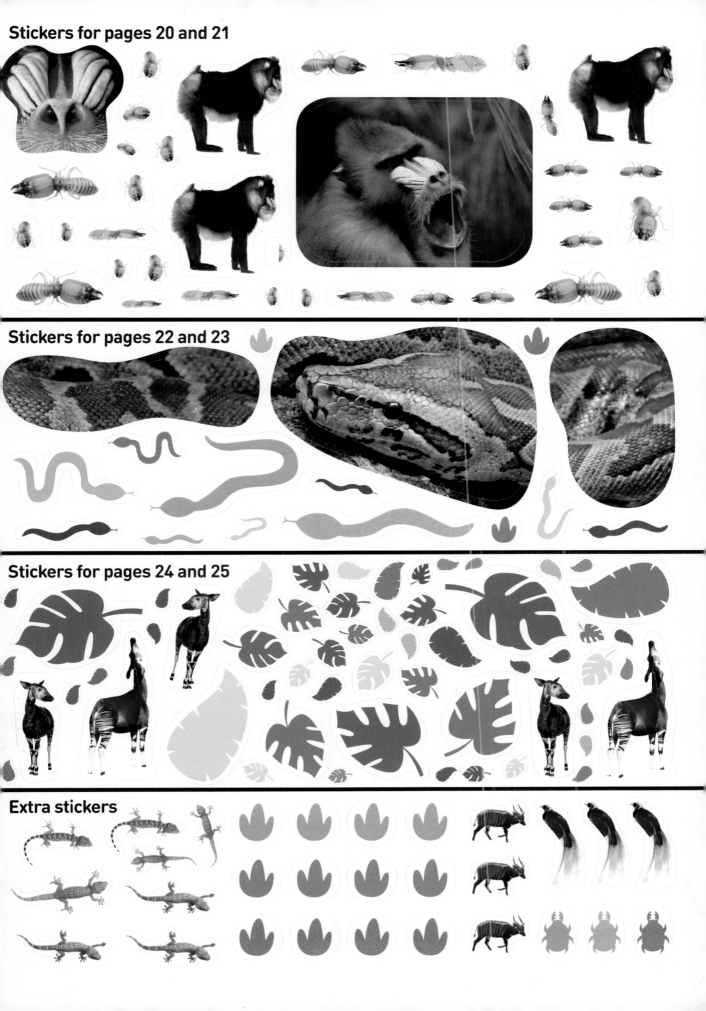

Stickers for pages 20 and 21

Stickers for pages 22 and 23

Stickers for pages 24 and 25

Extra stickers

Stickers for pages 26 and 27

Stickers for pages 28 and 29

Extra stickers

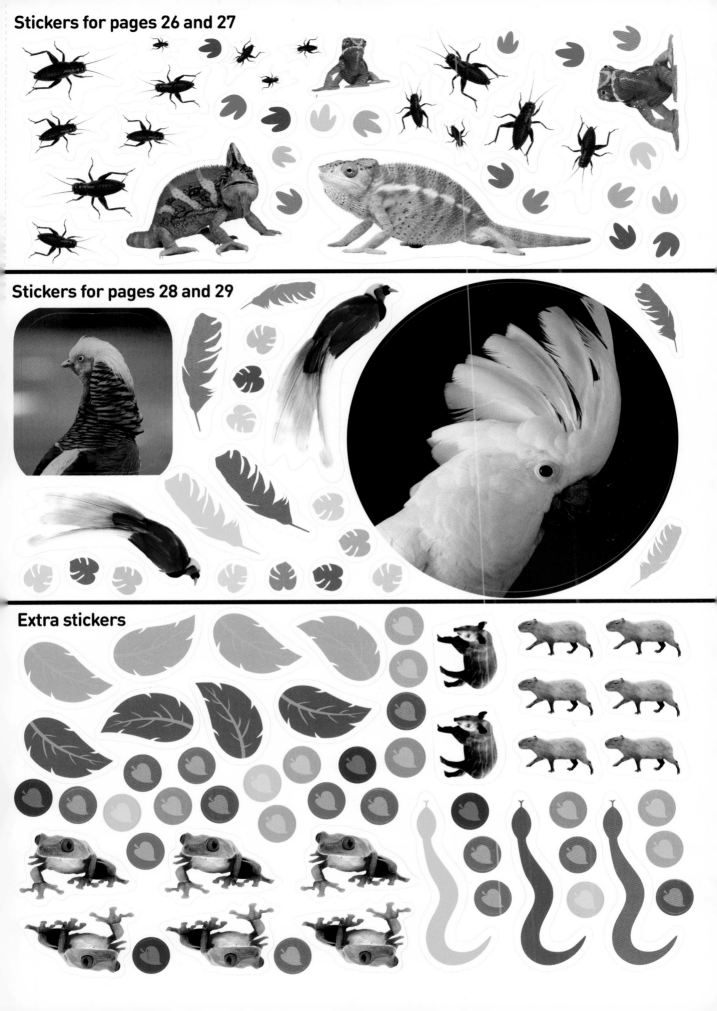

Sticker the missing mandrills, then find the one that's different!

When a mandrill shows its fearsome teeth, it is usually just being friendly!

Color the mandrill!

mandrill

Beware of the black mamba!

Black mambas are the fastest and most dangerous snakes in Africa.

black mambas

How many snakes can you count?

Look for the words to finish the word search.

m	h	i	s	s
a	k	z	n	w
m	d	p	a	l
b	e	y	k	v
a	t	g	e	u

hiss
mamba
snake

Color the snake!

Draw your own wiggly snake!

African rock pythons can swallow large animals such as monkeys and crocodiles!

African rock pythons

Find the missing stickers.

Okapis and bongos like to hide!

Striped coats help bongos and okapis blend into the forest.

Be a jungle explorer! How many animals can you count?

24

bongo

okapi

Okapis strip leaves from branches using their long, gripping tongues.

Sticker more leaves.

Draw the other half of the butterfly.

common blue charaxes butterfly

goliath beetle

Chameleons are colorful!

panther chameleon

Chameleons grip the treetop branches in the jungle using their toes.

Color your own chameleon.

Sticker bugs for the chameleon's lunch!

26

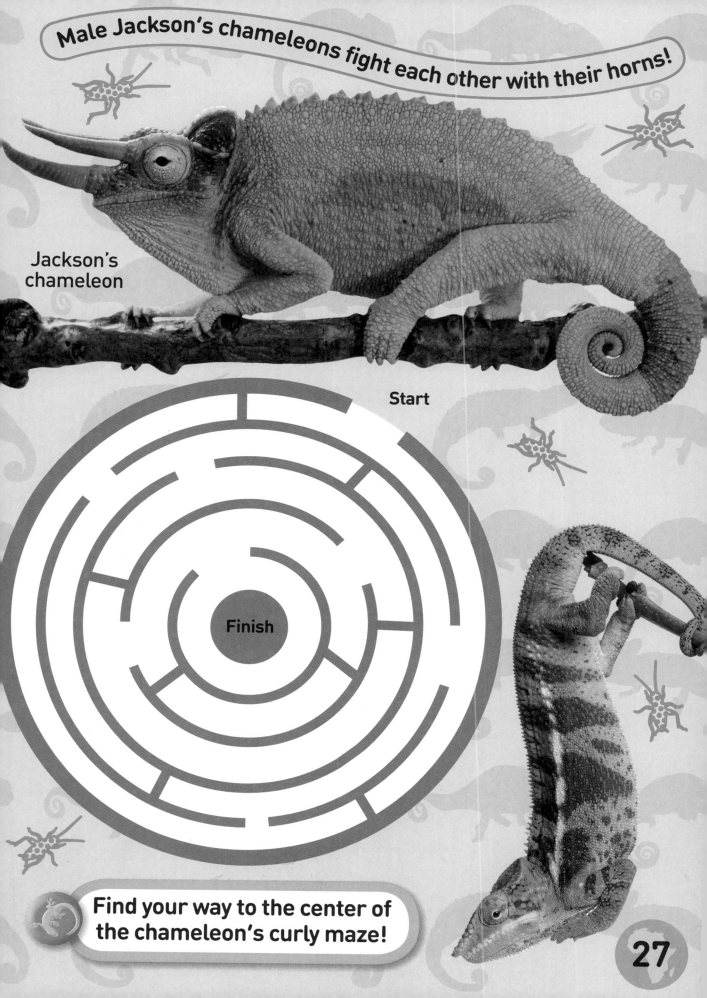

Male Jackson's chameleons fight each other with their horns!

Jackson's chameleon

Start

Finish

Find your way to the center of
the chameleon's curly maze!

27

These animals live in Asia.

Victoria crowned pigeon

The Victoria crowned pigeon is the largest living pigeon. It can be as big as a turkey!

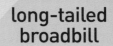

golden pheasant

long-tailed broadbill

Male birds of paradise try to attract females by performing dances!

Follow the trails to find out which bird wins!

The feathers on a cockatoo's head form a crest.

Color and sticker the cockatoos!

white umbrella cockatoo

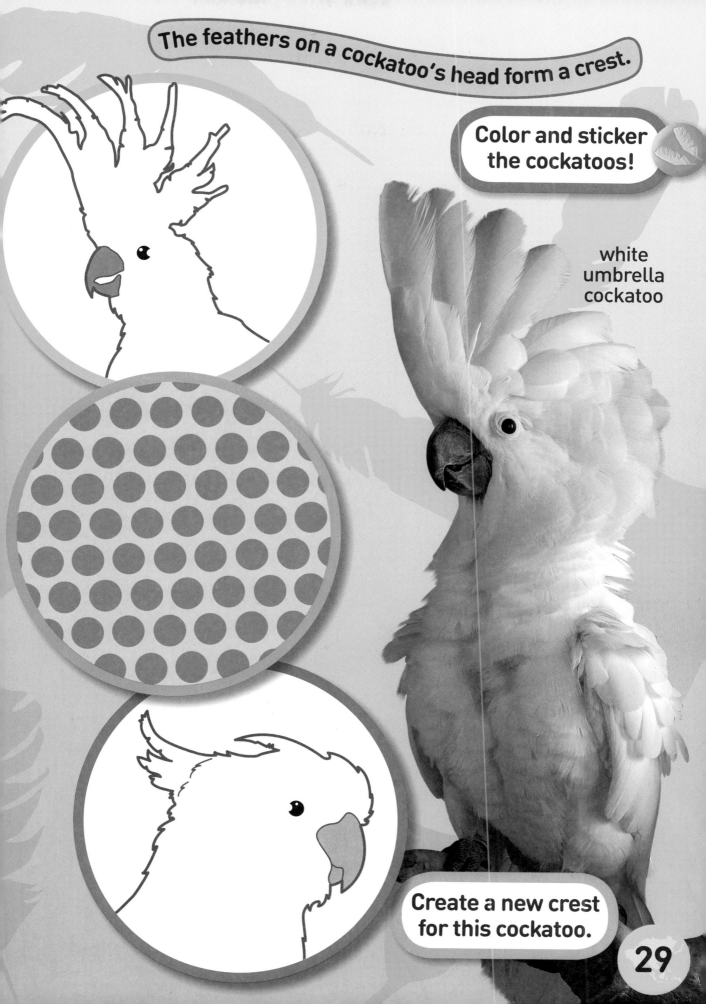

Create a new crest for this cockatoo.

Tigers prowl.

Find the missing stickers and circle the one that's different.

A tiger's stripes help it hide from its prey.

Color the grass to hide the tiger!

Use the grid to draw the tiger.

Sticker more paw prints on the tiger trail! How many can you count?

Tigers are great swimmers!

Life in the trees.

Sticker more bats!

A group of flying fox bats can contain thousands of bats! In the day, they rest upside down in tall trees.

flying fox bats

Use stickers to finish the bat sums!

3 + 2 = 5

1 + 3 = 4

Wallace's flying frog

Flying frogs don't actually fly. They spread out their webbed feet and glide through the air!

Sticker the frogs' webbed feet!

Draw your own amazing flying frog!

The world's largest tree frog is the white-lipped tree frog.

white-lipped tree frog

Amazing arowana fish!

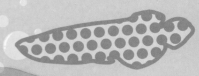

super red
arowana

Arowanas swim through jungle swamps and marshes.

red-tailed golden
arowana

Sticker more arowanas!

Find four differences between the fish!

A male arowana holds eggs in its mouth until the young are ready to hatch.

Sticker more bubbles!

Start

Finish

Help the fish find his babies.

35

Jungle **lizards** have spines and spots!

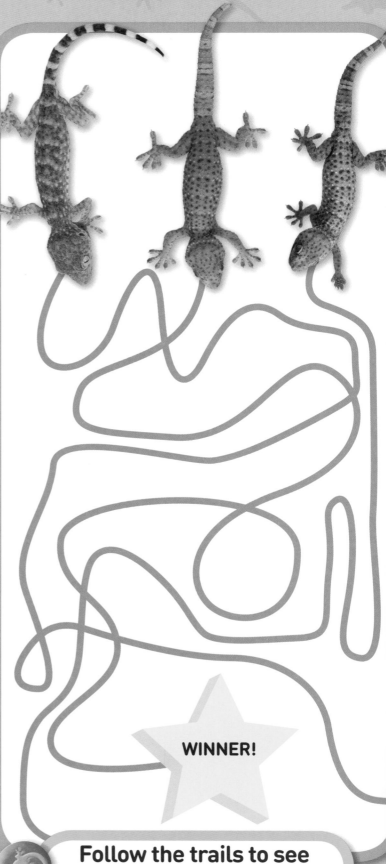

Tokay geckos are excellent at climbing up jungle trees!

WINNER!

Follow the trails to see who is the fastest climber!

Borneo anglehead lizards like to rest in the shade.

spines

The Borneo anglehead lizard has comblike spines that run from its neck to its tail!

Sticker more lizards!

Connect the dots and add color!

Color the lizard.

Borneo anglehead lizard

Swinging through the trees!

Orangutans and gibbons use their long arms to swing from tree to tree.

white-handed gibbon

orangutans

Orangutans are smart. They make leaf umbrellas to protect themselves from the rain.

Color the leaves.

Sticker a leaf umbrella!

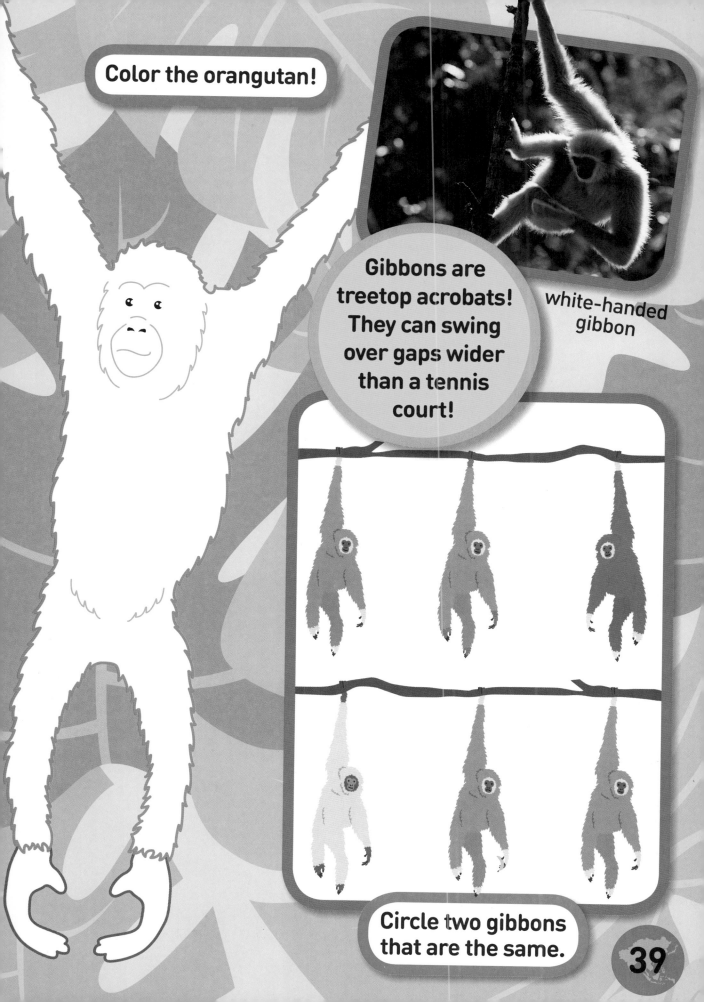

Color the orangutan!

white-handed gibbon

Gibbons are treetop acrobats! They can swing over gaps wider than a tennis court!

Circle two gibbons that are the same.

39

Jungle animals are awesome!

Sticker the jungle animals.

blue-and-yellow macaw

three-toed sloth

Draw your favorite jungle animal!

Sticker the jungle cats.

A macaw's bright feathers help it blend in with jungle leaves and fruits.

Color the snake.

tiger